The Ultimate Air Fryer Cookbook

Effortless Air Fryer Recipes for Beginners and Advanced Users

Bruna Ravenna

BREAKFAST 7

Shrimp Sandwiches 7

Breakfast Pea Tortilla 10

Raspberry Rolls 12

Potato and Leek Frittata 14

Espresso Oatmeal 16

Mushroom Oatmeal 18

Walnuts and Pear Oatmeal 20

LUNCH 22

Cinnamon and Cream Cheese Oats 23

Meatballs and Tomato Sauce 25

Stuffed Meatballs 27

Steaks and Cabbage 29

Succulent Lunch Turkey Breast 31

Italian Eggplant Sandwich 33

Creamy Chicken Stew 36

Lunch Pork and Potatoes 38

Turkey Cakes 40

SIDE DISHES 42

Garlic Potatoes 43

Eggplant Side Dish 45

Mushrooms and Sour Cream 47

Eggplant Fries 49

Fried Tomatoes 51

BREAKFAST

Shrimp Sandwiches

Preparation time: 10 minutes Cooking time: 5 minutes **Servings**: 4

Ingredients:

1 and ¼ cups cheddar, shredded

6 ounces canned tiny shrimp, drained

3 tablespoons mayonnaise

2 tablespoons green onions, chopped

4 whole wheat bread slices

2 tablespoons butter, soft

Directions:

1. In a bowl, mix shrimp with cheese, green onion and mayo and stir well.

2. Spread this on half of the bread slices, top with the other bread slices, cut

into halves diagonally and spread butter on top.

3. Place sandwiches in your air fryer and cook at 350 degrees F for 5

minutes.

4. Divide shrimp sandwiches on plates and serve them for breakfast.

Enjoy!

Nutrition: calories 162, fat 3, fiber 7, carbs 12, protein 4

Breakfast Pea Tortilla

Preparation time: 10 minutes Cooking time: 7

minutes **Servings**: 8

Ingredients:

½ pound baby peas

4 tablespoons butter

1 and ½ cup yogurt

8 eggs

½ cup mint, chopped

Salt and black pepper to the taste

Directions:

1. Heat up a pan that fits your air fryer with the

butter over medium heat,

add peas, stir and cook for a couple of minutes.

2. Meanwhile, in a bowl, mix half of the yogurt with

salt, pepper, eggs and

mint and whisk well.

3. Pour this over the peas, toss, introduce in your air

fryer and cook at 350

degrees F for 7 minutes.

4. Spread the rest of the yogurt over your tortilla, slice and serve.

Enjoy!

Nutrition: calories 192, fat 5, fiber 4, carbs 8, protein 7

Raspberry Rolls

Preparation time: 30 minutes Cooking time: 20 minutes **Servings**: 6

Ingredients:

1 cup milk

4 tablespoons butter

3 and ¼ cups flour

2 teaspoons yeast

¼ cup sugar

1 egg

For the filling:

8 ounces cream cheese, soft

12 ounces raspberries

1 teaspoons vanilla extract

5 tablespoons sugar

1 tablespoon cornstarch

Zest from 1 lemon, grated

Directions:

1. In a bowl, mix flour with sugar and yeast and stir.

2. Add milk and egg, stir until you obtain a dough, leave it aside to rise for

30 minutes, transfer dough to a working surface and roll well.

3. In a bowl, mix cream cheese with sugar, vanilla and lemon zest, stir well

and spread over dough.

4. In another bowl, mix raspberries with cornstarch, stir and spread over

cream cheese mix.

5. Roll your dough, cut into medium pieces, place them in your air fryer,

spray them with cooking spray and cook them at 350 degrees F for 30

minutes.

6. Serve your rolls for breakfast.

Enjoy!

Nutrition: calories 261, fat 5, fiber 8, carbs 9, protein 6

Potato and Leek Frittata

Preparation time: 10 minutes Cooking time: 18 minutes **Servings**: 4

Ingredients:

2 gold potatoes, boiled, peeled and chopped

2 tablespoons butter

2 leeks, sliced

Salt and black pepper to the taste

¼ cup whole milk

10 eggs, whisked

5 ounces fromage blanc, crumbled

Directions:

1. Heat up a pan that fits your air fryer with the butter over medium heat,
add leeks, stir and cook for 4 minutes.

2. Add potatoes, salt, pepper, eggs, cheese and milk, whisk well, cook for 1
minute more, introduce in your air fryer and cook at 350 degrees F for 13
minutes.

3. Slice frittata, divide among plates and serve. Enjoy!

Nutrition: calories 271, fat 6, fiber 8, carbs 12, protein 6

Espresso Oatmeal

Preparation time: 10 minutes Cooking time: 17

minutes **Servings**: 4

Ingredients:

1 cup milk

1 cup steel cut oats

2 and ½ cups water

2 tablespoons sugar

1 teaspoon espresso powder

2 teaspoons vanilla extract

Directions:

1. In a pan that fits your air fryer, mix oats with

water, sugar, milk and

espresso powder, stir, introduce in your air fryer and

cook at 360 degrees

F for 17 minutes.

2. Add vanilla extract, stir, leave everything aside for

5 minutes, divide into

bowls and serve for breakfast.

Enjoy!

Nutrition: calories 261, fat 7, fiber 6, carbs 39, protein 6

Mushroom Oatmeal

Preparation time: 10 minutes Cooking time: 20 minutes **Servings**: 4

Ingredients:

1 small yellow onion, chopped

1 cup steel cut oats

2 garlic cloves, minced

2 tablespoons butter

½ cup water

14 ounces canned chicken stock

3 thyme springs, chopped

2 tablespoons extra virgin olive oil

½ cup gouda cheese, grated

8 ounces mushroom, sliced

Salt and black pepper to the taste

Directions:

1. Heat up a pan that fits your air fryer with the butter over medium heat,

add onions and garlic, stir and cook for 4 minutes.

2. Add oats, water, salt, pepper, stock and thyme, stir, introduce in your air

fryer and cook at 360 degrees F for 16 minutes.

3. Meanwhile, heat up a pan with the olive oil over medium heat, add

mushrooms, cook them for 3 minutes, add to

oatmeal and cheese, stir,

divide into bowls and serve for breakfast.

Enjoy!

Nutrition: calories 284, fat 8, fiber 8, carbs 20,

protein 17

Walnuts and Pear Oatmeal

Preparation time: 5 minutes Cooking time: 12 minutes **Servings**: 4

Ingredients:

1 cup water

1 tablespoon butter, soft

¼ cups brown sugar

½ teaspoon cinnamon powder

1 cup rolled oats

½ cup walnuts, chopped

2 cups pear, peeled and chopped

½ cup raisins

Directions:

1. In a heat proof dish that fits your air fryer, mix milk with sugar, butter,

oats, cinnamon, raisins, pears and walnuts, stir, introduce in your fryer

and cook at 360 degrees F for 12 minutes.

2. Divide into bowls and serve.

Enjoy!

Nutrition: calories 230, fat 6, fiber 11, carbs 20, protein 5

LUNCH

Cinnamon and Cream Cheese Oats

Preparation time: 10 minutes Cooking time: 25

minutes **Servings**: 4

Ingredients:

1 cup steel oats

3 cups milk

1 tablespoon butter

¾ cup raisins

1 teaspoon cinnamon powder

¼ cup brown sugar

2 tablespoons white sugar

2 ounces cream cheese, soft

Directions:

1. Heat up a pan that fits your air fryer with the

butter over medium heat,

add oats, stir and toast them for 3 minutes.

2. Add milk and raisins, stir, introduce in your air

fryer and cook at 350

degrees F for 20 minutes.

3. Meanwhile, in a bowl, mix cinnamon with brown sugar and stir.

4. In a second bowl, mix white sugar with cream cheese and whisk.

5. Divide oats into bowls and top each with cinnamon and cream cheese.

Enjoy!

Nutrition: calories 152, fat 6, fiber 6, carbs 25, protein 7

Meatballs and Tomato Sauce

Preparation time: 10 minutes Cooking time: 15 minutes **Servings**: 4

Ingredients:

1 pound lean beef, ground

3 green onions, chopped

2 garlic cloves, minced

1 egg yolk

¼ cup bread crumbs

Salt and black pepper to the taste

1 tablespoon olive oil

16 ounces tomato sauce

2 tablespoons mustard

Directions:

1. In a bowl, mix beef with onion, garlic, egg yolk, bread crumbs, salt and

pepper, stir well and shape medium meatballs out of this mix.

2. Grease meatballs with the oil, place them in your air fryer and cook them

at 400 degrees F for 10 minutes.

3. In a bowl, mix tomato sauce with mustard, whisk, add over meatballs,

toss them and cook at 400 degrees F for 5 minutes more.

4. Divide meatballs and sauce on plates and serve for lunch.

Enjoy!

Nutrition: calories 300, fat 8, fiber 9, carbs 16, protein 5

Stuffed Meatballs

Preparation time: 10 minutes Cooking time: 10 minutes **Servings**: 4

Ingredients:

1/3 cup bread crumbs

3 tablespoons milk

1 tablespoon ketchup

1 egg

½ teaspoon marjoram, dried

Salt and black pepper to the taste

1 pound lean beef, ground

20 cheddar cheese cubes

1 tablespoon olive oil

Directions:

1. In a bowl, mix bread crumbs with ketchup, milk, marjoram, salt, pepper
and egg and whisk well.

2. Add beef, stir and shape 20 meatballs out of this mix.

3. Shape each meatball around a cheese cube, drizzle the oil over them and
rub.
4. Place all meatballs in your preheated air fryer and cook at 390 degrees F
for 10 minutes.
5. Serve them for lunch with a side salad.
Enjoy!
Nutrition: calories 200, fat 5, fiber 8, carbs 12, protein 5

Steaks and Cabbage

Preparation time: 10 minutes Cooking time: 10

minutes **Servings**: 4

Ingredients:

½ pound sirloin steak, cut into strips

2 teaspoons cornstarch

1 tablespoon peanut oil

2 cups green cabbage, chopped

1 yellow bell pepper, chopped

2 green onions, chopped

2 garlic cloves, minced

Salt and black pepper to the taste

Directions:

1. In a bowl, mix cabbage with salt, pepper and

peanut oil, toss, transfer to

air fryer's basket, cook at 370 degrees F for 4 minutes

and transfer to a

bowl.

2. Add steak strips to your air fryer, also add green

onions, bell pepper,

garlic, salt and pepper, toss and cook for 5 minutes.
3. Add over cabbage, toss, divide among plates and serve for lunch.

Enjoy!

Nutrition: calories 282, fat 6, fiber 8, carbs 14, protein 6

Succulent Lunch Turkey Breast

Preparation time: 10 minutes Cooking time: 47 minutes **Servings**: 4

Ingredients:

1 big turkey breast

2 teaspoons olive oil

½ teaspoon smoked paprika

1 teaspoon thyme, dried

½ teaspoon sage, dried

Salt and black pepper to the taste

2 tablespoons mustard

¼ cup maple syrup

1 tablespoon butter, soft

Directions:

1. Brush turkey breast with the olive oil, season with salt, pepper, thyme,

paprika and sage, rub, place in your air fryer's basket and fry at 350

degrees F for 25 minutes.

2. Flip turkey, cook for 10 minutes more, flip one more time and cook for

another 10 minutes.

3. Meanwhile, heat up a pan with the butter over medium heat, add mustard

and maple syrup, stir well, cook for a couple of minutes and take off heat.

4. Slice turkey breast, divide among plates and serve with the maple glaze

drizzled on top.

Enjoy!

Nutrition: calories 280, fat 2, fiber 7, carbs 16, protein 14

Italian Eggplant Sandwich

Preparation time: 10 minutes Cooking time: 16 minutes **Servings**: 2

Ingredients:

1 eggplant, sliced

2 teaspoons parsley, dried

Salt and black pepper to the taste

½ cup breadcrumbs

½ teaspoon Italian seasoning

½ teaspoon garlic powder

½ teaspoon onion powder

2 tablespoons milk

4 bread slices

Cooking spray

½ cup mayonnaise

¾ cup tomato sauce

2 cups mozzarella cheese, grated

Directions:

1. Season eggplant slices with salt and pepper, leave aside for 10

minutes and then pat dry them well.

2. In a bowl, mix parsley with breadcrumbs, Italian seasoning, onion

and garlic powder, salt and black pepper and stir.

3. In another bowl, mix milk with mayo and whisk well.

4. Brush eggplant slices with mayo mix, dip them in breadcrumbs,

place them in your air fryer's basket, spray with cooking oil and

cook them at 400 degrees F for 15 minutes, flipping them after 8

minutes.

5. Brush each bread slice with olive oil and arrange 2 on a working

surface.

6. Add mozzarella and parmesan on each, add baked eggplant slices,

spread tomato sauce and basil and top with the other bread slices, greased side down.

7. Divide sandwiches on plates, cut them in halves and serve for

lunch.

Enjoy!**Nutrition**: calories 324, fat 16, fiber 4, carbs 39, protein 12

Creamy Chicken Stew

Preparation time: 10 minutes Cooking time: 25

minutes **Servings**: 4

Ingredients:

1 and ½ cups canned cream of celery soup

6 chicken tenders

Salt and black pepper to the taste

2 potatoes, chopped

1 bay leaf

1 thyme spring, chopped

1 tablespoon milk

1 egg yolk

½ cup heavy cream

Directions:

1. In a bowl, mix chicken with cream of celery,

potatoes, heavy

cream, bay leaf, thyme, salt and pepper, toss, pour

into your air

fryer's pan and cook at 320 degrees F for 25 minutes.

2. Leave your stew to cool down a bit, discard bay leaf, divide among

plates and serve right away.

Enjoy!

Nutrition: calories 300, fat 11, fiber 2, carbs 23, protein 14

Lunch Pork and Potatoes

Preparation time: 10 minutes Cooking time: 25 minutes **Servings**: 2

Ingredients:

2 pounds pork loin

Salt and black pepper to the taste

2 red potatoes, cut into medium wedges

½ teaspoon garlic powder

½ teaspoon red pepper flakes

1 teaspoon parsley, dried

A drizzle of balsamic vinegar

Directions:

1. In your air fryer's pan, mix pork with potatoes, salt, pepper, garlic

powder, pepper flakes, parsley and vinegar, toss and cook at 390

degrees F for 25 minutes.

2. Slice pork, divide it and potatoes on plates and serve for lunch.

Enjoy!

Nutrition: calories 400, fat 15, fiber 7, carbs 27, protein 20

Turkey Cakes

Preparation time: 10 minutes Cooking time: 10 minutes **Servings**: 4

Ingredients:

6 mushrooms, chopped

1 teaspoon garlic powder

1 teaspoon onion powder

Salt and black pepper to the taste

1 and ¼ pounds turkey meat, ground

Cooking spray

Tomato sauce for serving

Directions:

1. In your blender, mix mushrooms with salt and pepper, pulse well

and transfer to a bowl.

2. Add turkey, onion powder, garlic powder, salt and pepper, stir and

shape cakes out of this mix.

3. Spray them with cooking spray, transfer them to your air fryer and

cook at 320 degrees F for 10 minutes.

4. Serve them with tomato sauce on the side and a tasty side salad.

Enjoy!

Nutrition: calories 202, fat 6, fiber 3, carbs 17, protein 10

SIDE DISHES

Garlic Potatoes

Preparation time: 10 minutes Cooking time: 20 minutes **Servings**: 6

Ingredients:

2 tablespoons parsley, chopped

5 garlic cloves, minced

½ teaspoon basil, dried

½ teaspoon oregano, dried

3 pounds red potatoes, halved

1 teaspoon thyme, dried

2 tablespoons olive oil

Salt and black pepper to the taste

2 tablespoons butter

1/3 cup parmesan, grated

Directions:

1. In a bowl, mix potato halves with parsley, garlic, basil, oregano, thyme,

salt, pepper, oil and butter, toss really well and transfer to your air fryer's

basket.

2. Cover and cook at 400 degrees F for 20 minutes, flipping them once.

3. Sprinkle parmesan on top, divide potatoes on plates and serve as a side dish.

Enjoy!

Nutrition: calories 162, fat 5, fiber 5, carbs 7, protein 5

Eggplant Side Dish

Preparation time: 10 minutes Cooking time: 10 minutes **Servings**: 4

Ingredients:

8 baby eggplants, scooped in the center and pulp reserved

Salt and black pepper to the taste

A pinch of oregano, dried

1 green bell pepper, chopped

1 tablespoon tomato paste

1 bunch coriander, chopped

½ teaspoon garlic powder

1 tablespoon olive oil

1 yellow onion, chopped

1 tomato chopped

Directions:

1. Heat up a pan with the oil over medium heat, add onion, stir and cook for

1 minute.

2. Add salt, pepper, eggplant pulp, oregano, green bell pepper, tomato paste,
garlic power, coriander and tomato, stir, cook for 1-2 minutes more, take
off heat and cool down.
3. Stuff eggplants with this mix, place them in your air fryer's basket and
cook at 360 degrees F for 8 minutes.
4. Divide eggplants on plates and serve them as a side dish.
Enjoy!
Nutrition: calories 200, fat 3, fiber 7, carbs 12, protein 4

Mushrooms and Sour Cream

Preparation time: 10 minutes Cooking time: 10 minutes **Servings**: 6

Ingredients:

2 bacon strips, chopped

1 yellow onion, chopped

1 green bell pepper, chopped

24 mushrooms, stems removed

1 carrot, grated

½ cup sour cream

1 cup cheddar cheese, grated

Salt and black pepper to the taste

Directions:

1. Heat up a pan over medium high heat, add bacon, onion, bell pepper and
carrot, stir and cook for 1 minute.

2. Add salt, pepper and sour cream, stir cook for 1 minute more, take off
heat and cool down.

3. Stuff mushrooms with this mix, sprinkle cheese on

top and cook at 360

degrees F for 8 minutes.

4. Divide among plates and serve as a side dish.

Enjoy!

Nutrition: calories 211, fat 4, fiber 7, carbs 8, protein

3

Eggplant Fries

Preparation time: 10 minutes Cooking time: 5

minutes **Servings**: 4

Ingredients:

Cooking spray

1 eggplant, peeled and cut into medium fries

2 tablespoons milk

1 egg, whisked

2 cups panko bread crumbs

½ cup Italian cheese, shredded

A pinch of salt and black pepper to the taste

Directions:

1. In a bowl, mix egg with milk, salt and pepper and

whisk well.

2. In another bowl, mix panko with cheese and stir.

3. Dip eggplant fries in egg mix, then coat in panko

mix, place them in your

air fryer greased with cooking spray and cook at 400

degrees F for 5

minutes.

4. Divide among plates and serve as a side dish.

Enjoy!

Nutrition: calories 162, fat 5, fiber 5, carbs 7, protein 6

Fried Tomatoes

Preparation time: 10 minutes Cooking time: 5

minutes **Servings**: 4

Ingredients:

2 green tomatoes, sliced

Salt and black pepper to the taste

½ cup flour

1 cup buttermilk

1 cup panko bread crumbs

½ tablespoon Creole seasoning

Cooking spray

Directions:

1. Season tomato slices with salt and pepper.

2. Put flour in a bowl, buttermilk in another and

panko crumbs and Creole

seasoning in a third one.

3. Dredge tomato slices in flour, then in buttermilk

and panko bread crumbs,

place them in your air fryer's basket greased with

cooking spray and cook

them at 400 degrees F for 5 minutes.

4. Divide among plates and serve as a side dish.

Enjoy!

Nutrition: calories 124, fat 5, fiber 7, carbs 9, protein 4

Cauliflower Cakes

Preparation time: 10 minutes Cooking time: 10 minutes **Servings**: 6

Ingredients:

3 and ½ cups cauliflower rice

2 eggs

¼ cup white flour

½ cup parmesan, grated

Salt and black pepper to the taste

Cooking spray

Directions:

1. In a bowl, mix cauliflower rice with salt and pepper, stir and squeeze
excess water.

2. Transfer cauliflower to another bowl, add eggs, salt, pepper, flour and
parmesan, stir really well and shape your cakes.

3. Grease your air fryer with cooking spray, heat it up at 400 degrees, add

cauliflower cakes and cook them for 10 minutes flipping them halfway.

4. Divide cakes on plates and serve as a side dish. Enjoy!

Nutrition: calories 125, fat 2, fiber 6, carbs 8, protein 3

Creamy Brussels Sprouts

Preparation time: 10 minutes Cooking time: 25

minutes **Servings**: 8

Ingredients:

3 pounds Brussels sprouts, halved

A drizzle of olive oil

1 pound bacon, chopped

Salt and black pepper to the taste

4 tablespoons butter

3 shallots, chopped

1 cup milk

2 cups heavy cream

¼ teaspoon nutmeg, ground

3 tablespoons prepared horseradish

Directions:

1. Preheated you air fryer at 370 degrees F, add oil,

bacon, salt and pepper

and Brussels sprouts and toss.

2. Add butter, shallots, heavy cream, milk, nutmeg

and horseradish, toss

again and cook for 25 minutes.

3. Divide among plates and serve as a side dish.

Enjoy!

Nutrition: calories 214, fat 5, fiber 8, carbs 12,

protein 5

Cheddar Biscuits

Preparation time: 10 minutes Cooking time: 20 minutes **Servings**: 8

Ingredients:

2 and 1/3 cup self-rising flour

½ cup butter+ 1 tablespoon, melted

2 tablespoons sugar

½ cup cheddar cheese, grated

1 and 1/3 cup buttermilk

1 cup flour

Directions:

1. In a bowl, mix self-rising flour with ½ cup butter, sugar, cheddar cheese
and buttermilk and stir until you obtain a dough.

2. Spread 1 cup flour on a working surface, roll dough, flatten it, cut 8
circles with a cookie cutter and coat them with flour.

3. Line your air fryer's basket with tin foil, add biscuits, brush them with

melted butter and cook them at 380 degrees F for 20 minutes.

4. Divide among plates and serve as a side. Enjoy!

Nutrition: calories 221, fat 3, fiber 8, carbs 12, protein 4

Zucchini Fries

Preparation time: 10 minutes Cooking time: 12

minutes **Servings**: 4

Ingredients:

1 zucchini, cut into medium sticks

A drizzle of olive oil

Salt and black pepper to the taste

2 eggs, whisked

1 cup bread crumbs

½ cup flour

Directions:

1. Put flour in a bowl and mix with salt and pepper

and stir.

2. Put breadcrumbs in another bowl.

3. In a third bowl mix eggs with a pinch of salt and

pepper.

4. Dredge zucchini fries in flour, then in eggs and in

bread crumbs at the

end.

5. Grease your air fryer with some olive oil, heat up at 400 degrees F, add

zucchini fries and cook them for 12 minutes.

6. Serve them as a side dish.

Enjoy!

Nutrition: calories 172, fat 3, fiber 3, carbs 7, protein 3

Cheesy Artichokes

Preparation time: 10 minutes Cooking time: 6

minutes **Servings**: 6

Ingredients:

14 ounces canned artichoke hearts

8 ounces cream cheese

16 ounces parmesan cheese, grated

10 ounces spinach

½ cup chicken stock

8 ounces mozzarella, shredded

½ cup sour cream

3 garlic cloves, minced

½ cup mayonnaise

1 teaspoon onion powder

Directions:

1. In a pan that fits your air fryer, mix artichokes with

stock, garlic,

spinach, cream cheese, sour cream, onion powder

and mayo, toss,

introduce in your air fryer and cook at 350 degrees F for 6 minutes.

2. Add mozzarella and parmesan, stir well and serve. Enjoy!

Nutrition: calories 261, fat 12, fiber 2, carbs 12, protein 15

Artichokes and Special Sauce

Preparation time: 10 minutes Cooking time: 6

minutes **Servings**: 2

Ingredients:

2 artichokes, trimmed

A drizzle of olive oil

2 garlic cloves, minced

1 tablespoon lemon juice

For the sauce:

¼ cup coconut oil

¼ cup extra virgin olive oil

3 anchovy fillets

3 garlic cloves

Directions:

1. In a bowl, mix artichokes with oil, 2 garlic cloves

and lemon juice, toss

well, transfer to your air fryer, cook at 350 degrees F

for 6 minutes and

divide among plates.

2. In your food processor, mix coconut oil with anchovy, 3 garlic cloves and

olive oil, blend very well, drizzle over artichokes and serve.

Enjoy!

Nutrition: calories 261, fat 4, fiber 7, carbs 20, protein 12

Beet Salad and Parsley Dressing

Preparation time: 10 minutes Cooking time: 14 minutes **Servings**: 4

Ingredients:

4 beets

2 tablespoons balsamic vinegar

A bunch of parsley, chopped

Salt and black pepper to the taste

1 tablespoon extra virgin olive oil

1 garlic clove, chopped

2 tablespoons capers

Directions:

1. Put beets in your air fryer and cook them at 360 degrees F for 14

minutes.

2. Meanwhile, in a bowl, mix parsley with garlic, salt, pepper, olive

oil and capers and stir very well.

3. Transfer beets to a cutting board, leave them to cool down, peel

them, slice put them in a salad bowl.

4. Add vinegar, drizzle the parsley dressing all over and serve.

Enjoy!

Nutrition: calories 70, fat 2, fiber 1, carbs 6, protein 4

Beets and Blue Cheese Salad

Preparation time: 10 minutes Cooking time: 14 minutes **Servings**: 6

Ingredients:

6 beets, peeled and quartered

Salt and black pepper to the taste

¼ cup blue cheese, crumbled

1 tablespoon olive oil

Directions:

1. Put beets in your air fryer, cook them at 350 degrees F for 14 minutes and transfer them to a bowl.

2. Add blue cheese, salt, pepper and oil, toss and serve.

Enjoy!

Nutrition: calories 100, fat 4, fiber 4, carbs 10, protein 5

Beet s and Arugula Salad

Preparation time: 10 minutes Cooking time: 10 minutes **Servings**: 4

Ingredients:

1 and ½ pounds beets, peeled and quartered

A drizzle of olive oil

2 teaspoons orange zest, grated

2 tablespoons cider vinegar

½ cup orange juice

2 tablespoons brown sugar

2 scallions, chopped

2 teaspoons mustard

2 cups arugula

Directions:

1. Rub beets with the oil and orange juice, place them in your air

fryer and cook at 350 degrees F for 10 minutes.

2. Transfer beet quarters to a bowl, add scallions, arugula and orange

zest and toss.

3. In a separate bowl, mix sugar with mustard and vinegar, whisk

well, add to salad, toss and serve.

Enjoy!

Nutrition: calories 121, fat 2, fiber 3, carbs 11, protein 4

MEAT

Chinese Stuffed Chicke n

Preparation time: 10 minutes Cooking time: 35
minutes **Servings**: 8

Ingredients:

1 whole chicken

10 wolfberries

2 red chilies, chopped

4 ginger slices

1 yam, cubed

1 teaspoon soy sauce

Salt and white pepper to the taste

3 teaspoons sesame oil

Directions:

1. Season chicken with salt, pepper, rub with soy
sauce and sesame
oil and stuff with wolfberries, yam cubes, chilies and
ginger.

2. Place in your air fryer, cook at 400 degrees F for 20
minutes and
then at 360 degrees F for 15 minutes.

3. Carve chicken, divide among plates and serve. Enjoy!

Nutrition: calories 320, fat 12, fiber 17, carbs 22, protein 12

Easy Chicken Thighs and Baby Potatoes

Preparation time: 10 minutes Cooking time: 30 minutes **Servings**: 4

Ingredients:

8 chicken thighs

2 tablespoons olive oil

1 pound baby potatoes, halved

2 teaspoons oregano, dried

2 teaspoons rosemary, dried

½ teaspoon sweet paprika

Salt and black pepper to the taste

2 garlic cloves, minced

1 red onion, chopped

2 teaspoons thyme, chopped

Directions:

1. In a bowl, mix chicken thighs with potatoes, salt, pepper, thyme,

paprika, onion, rosemary, garlic, oregano and oil.

2. Toss to coat, spread everything in a heat proof dish that fits your

air fryer and cook at 400 degrees F for 30 minutes, shaking

halfway.

3. Divide among plates and serve.

Enjoy!

Nutrition: calories 364, fat 14, fiber 13, carbs 21, protein 34

Chicken and Capers

Preparation time: 10 minutes Cooking time: 20 minutes **Servings**: 2

Ingredients:

4 chicken thighs

3 tablespoons capers

4 garlic cloves, minced

3 tablespoons butter, melted

Salt and black pepper to the taste

½ cup chicken stock

1 lemon, sliced

4 green onions, chopped

Directions:

1. Brush chicken with butter, sprinkle salt and pepper to the taste,

place them in a baking dish that fits your air fryer.

2. Also add capers, garlic, chicken stock and lemon slices, toss to

coat, introduce in your air fryer and cook at 370 degrees F for 20 minutes, shaking halfway.

3. Sprinkle green onions, divide among plates and serve.

Enjoy!

Nutrition: calories 200, fat 9, fiber 10, carbs 17, protein 7

Chicken and Creamy Mushrooms

Preparation time: 10 minutes Cooking time: 30 minutes **Servings**: 8

Ingredients:

8 chicken thighs

Salt and black pepper to the taste

8 ounces cremini mushrooms, halved

3 garlic cloves, minced

3 tablespoons butter, melted

1 cup chicken stock

¼ cup heavy cream

½ teaspoon basil, dried

½ teaspoon thyme, dried

½ teaspoon oregano, dried

1 tablespoon mustard

¼ cup parmesan, grated

Directions:

1. Rub chicken pieces with 2 tablespoons butter, season with salt and

pepper, put in your air fryer's basket, cook at 370 degrees F for 5

minutes and leave aside in a bowl for now.

2. Meanwhile, heat up a pan with the rest of the butter over medium

high heat, add mushrooms and garlic, stir and cook for 5 minutes.

3. Add salt, pepper, stock, oregano, thyme and basil, stir well and

transfer to a heat proof dish that fits your air fryer.

4. Add chicken, toss everything, put in your air fryer and cook at 370

degrees F for 20 minutes.

5. Add mustard, parmesan and heavy cream, toss everything again,

cook for 5 minutes more, divide among plates and serve.

Enjoy!

Nutrition: calories 340, fat 10, fiber 13, carbs 22, protein 12Duck and Plum Sauce

Preparation time: 10 minutes Cooking time: 32

minutes **Servings**: 2

Ingredients:

2 duck breasts

1 tablespoon butter, melted

1 star anise

1 tablespoon olive oil

1 shallot, chopped

9 ounces red plumps, stoned, cut into small wedges

2 tablespoons sugar

2 tablespoons red wine

1 cup beef stock

Directions:

1. Heat up a pan with the olive oil over medium heat, add shallot, stir

and cook for 5 minutes,

2. Add sugar and plums, stir and cook until sugar dissolves.

3. Add stock and wine, stir, cook for 15 minutes, take off heat and

keep warm for now.

4. Score duck breasts, season with salt and pepper, rub with melted
butter, transfer to a heat proof dish that fits your air fryer, add star
anise and plum sauce, introduce in your air fryer and cook at 360
degrees F for 12 minutes.

5. Divide everything on plates and serve.

Enjoy!

Nutrition: calories 400, fat 25, fiber 12, carbs 29, protein 44

Air Fried Japanese Duck Breasts

Preparation time: 10 minutes Cooking time: 20 minutes **Servings**: 6

Ingredients:

6 duck breasts, boneless

4 tablespoons soy sauce

1 and ½ teaspoon five spice powder

2 tablespoons honey

Salt and black pepper to the taste

20 ounces chicken stock

4 ginger slices

4 tablespoons hoisin sauce

1 teaspoon sesame oil

Directions:

1. In a bowl, mix five spice powder with soy sauce, salt, pepper and

honey, whisk, add duck breasts, toss to coat and leave aside for

now.

2. Heat up a pan with the stock over medium high heat, hoisin sauce,

ginger and sesame oil, stir well, cook for 2-3 minutes more, take

off heat and leave aside.

3. Put duck breasts in your air fryer and cook them at 400 degrees F

for 15 minutes.

4. Divide among plates, drizzle hoisin and ginger sauce all over them

and serve.

Enjoy!

Nutrition: calories 336, fat 12, fiber 1, carbs 25, protein 33

Easy Duck Breasts

Preparation time: 10 minutes Cooking time: 40 minutes **Servings**: 6

Ingredients:

6 duck breasts, halved

Salt and black pepper to the taste

3 tablespoons flour

6 tablespoons butter, melted

2 cups chicken stock

½ cup white wine

¼ cup parsley, chopped

2 cups mushrooms, chopped

Directions:

1. Season duck breasts with salt and pepper, place them in a bowl,

add melted butter, toss and transfer to another bowl.

2. Combine melted butter with flour, wine, salt, pepper and chicken

stock and stir well.

3. Arrange duck breasts in a baking dish that fits your air fryer, pour

the sauce over them, add parsley and mushrooms, introduce in your

air fryer and cook at 350 degrees F for 40 minutes.

4. Divide among plates and serve.

Enjoy!

Nutrition: calories 320, fat 28, fiber 12, carbs 12, protein 42

Duck Breasts with Endives

Preparation time: 10 minutes Cooking time: 25

minutes **Servings**: 4

Ingredients:

2 duck breasts

Salt and black pepper to the taste

1 tablespoon sugar

1 tablespoon olive oil

6 endives, julienned

2 tablespoons cranberries

8 ounces white wine

1 tablespoons garlic, minced

2 tablespoons heavy cream

Directions:

1. Score duck breasts and season them with salt and

pepper, put in

preheated air fryer and cook at 350 degrees F for 20

minutes,

flipping them halfway.

2. Meanwhile, heat up a pan with the oil over medium heat, add sugar
and endives, stir and cook for 2 minutes.

3. Add salt, pepper, wine, garlic, cream and cranberries, stir and cook
for 3 minutes.

4. Divide duck breasts on plates, drizzle the endives sauce all over
and serve.

Enjoy!

Nutrition: calories 400, fat 12, fiber 32, carbs 29, protein 28

Chicken Breasts and Tomatoes Sauce

Preparation time: 10 minutes Cooking time: 20 minutes **Servings**: 4

Ingredients:

1 red onion, chopped

4 chicken breasts, skinless and boneless

¼ cup balsamic vinegar

14 ounces canned tomatoes, chopped

Salt and black pepper to the taste

¼ cup parmesan, grated

¼ teaspoon garlic powder

Cooking spray

Directions:

1. Spray a baking dish that fits your air fryer with cooking oil, add

chicken, season with salt, pepper, balsamic vinegar, garlic powder,

tomatoes and cheese, toss, introduce in your air fryer and cook at

400 degrees F for 20 minutes.

2. Divide among plates and serve hot.

Enjoy!

Nutrition: calories 250, fat 12, fiber 12, carbs 19, protein 28

Chicken and Asparagus

Preparation time: 10 minutes Cooking time: 20

minutes **Servings**: 4

Ingredients:

8 chicken wings, halved

8 asparagus spears

Salt and black pepper to the taste

1 tablespoon rosemary, chopped

1 teaspoon cumin, ground

Directions:

1. Pat dry chicken wings, season with salt, pepper,

cumin and

rosemary, put them in your air fryer's basket and

cook at 360

degrees F for 20 minutes.

2. Meanwhile, heat up a pan over medium heat, add

asparagus, add

water to cover, steam for a few minutes, transfer to a

bowl filled

with ice water, drain and arrange on plates.

3. Add chicken wings on the side and serve.

Enjoy!

Nutrition: calories 270, fat 8, fiber 12, carbs 24, protein 22

Veggie

Apple Bread

Preparation time: 10 minutes Cooking time: 40

minutes **Servings**: 6

Ingredients:

3 cups apples, cored and cubed

1 cup sugar

1 tablespoon vanilla

2 eggs

1 tablespoon apple pie spice

2 cups white flour

1 tablespoon baking powder

1 stick butter

1 cup water

Directions:

1. In a bowl mix egg with 1 butter stick, apple pie

spice and sugar and

stir using your mixer.

2. Add apples and stir again well.

3. In another bowl, mix baking powder with flour

and stir.

4. Combine the 2 mixtures, stir and pour into a spring form pan.

5. Put spring form pan in your air fryer and cook at 320 degrees F for

40 minutes

6. Slice and serve.

Enjoy!

Nutrition: calories 192, fat 6, fiber 7, carbs 14, protein 7

Banana Bread

Preparation time: 10 minutes Cooking time: 40

minutes **Servings**: 6

Ingredients:

¾ cup sugar

1/3 cup butter

1 teaspoon vanilla extract

1 egg

2 bananas, mashed

1 teaspoon baking powder

1 and ½ cups flour

½ teaspoons baking soda

1/3 cup milk

1 and ½ teaspoons cream of tartar

Cooking spray

Directions:

1. In a bowl, mix milk with cream of tartar, sugar,

butter, egg, vanilla

and bananas and stir everything.

2. In another bowl, mix flour with baking powder and baking soda.

3. Combine the 2 mixtures, stir well, pour this into a cake pan greased

with some cooking spray, introduce in your air fryer and cook at

320 degrees F for 40 minutes.

4. Take bread out, leave aside to cool down, slice and serve it.

Enjoy!

Nutrition: calories 292, fat 7, fiber 8, carbs 28, protein 4

Mini Lava Cakes

Preparation time: 10 minutes Cooking time: 20

minutes **Servings**: 3

Ingredients:

1 egg

4 tablespoons sugar

2 tablespoons olive oil

4 tablespoons milk

4 tablespoons flour

1 tablespoon cocoa powder

½ teaspoon baking powder

½ teaspoon orange zest

Directions:

1. In a bowl, mix egg with sugar, oil, milk, flour, salt,

cocoa powder,

baking powder and orange zest, stir very well and

pour this into

greased ramekins.

2. Add ramekins to your air fryer and cook at 320

degrees F for 20

minutes.

3. Serve lava cakes warm.

Enjoy!

Nutrition: calories 201, fat 7, fiber 8, carbs 23, protein 4

Crispy Apple s

Preparation time: 10 minutes Cooking time: 10 minutes **Servings**: 4

Ingredients:

2 teaspoons cinnamon powder

5 apples, cored and cut into chunks

½ teaspoon nutmeg powder

1 tablespoon maple syrup

½ cup water

4 tablespoons butter

¼ cup flour

¾ cup old fashioned rolled oats

¼ cup brown sugar

Directions:

1. Put the apples in a pan that fits your air fryer, add cinnamon,

nutmeg, maple syrup and water.

2. In a bowl, mix butter with oats, sugar, salt and flour, stir, drop

spoonfuls of this mix on top of apples, introduce in your air fryer

and cook at 350 degrees F for 10 minutes.

3. Serve warm.

Enjoy!

Nutrition: calories 200, fat 6, fiber 8, carbs 29, protein 12

Carrot Cake

Preparation time: 10 minutes Cooking time: 45 minutes **Servings**: 6

Ingredients:

5 ounces flour

¾ teaspoon baking powder

½ teaspoon baking soda

½ teaspoon cinnamon powder

¼ teaspoon nutmeg, ground

½ teaspoon allspice

1 egg

3 tablespoons yogurt

½ cup sugar

¼ cup pineapple juice

4 tablespoons sunflower oil

1/3 cup carrots, grated

1/3 cup pecans, toasted and chopped

1/3 cup coconut flakes, shredded

Cooking spray

Directions:

1. In a bowl, mix flour with baking soda and powder, salt, allspice,

cinnamon and nutmeg and stir.

2. In another bowl, mix egg with yogurt, sugar, pineapple juice, oil, carrots,

pecans and coconut flakes and stir well.

3. Combine the two mixtures and stir well, pour this into a spring form pan

that fits your air fryer which you've greased with some cooking spray,

transfer to your air fryer and cook on 320 degrees F for 45 minutes.

4. Leave cake to cool down, then cut and serve it. Enjoy!

Nutrition: calories 200, fat 6, fiber 20, carbs 22, protein 4

Ginger Cheesecake

Preparation time: 2 hours and 10 minutes Cooking time: 20 minutes **Servings**:

6

Ingredients:

2 teaspoons butter, melted

½ cup ginger cookies, crumbled

16 ounces cream cheese, soft

2 eggs

½ cup sugar

1 teaspoon rum

½ teaspoon vanilla extract

½ teaspoon nutmeg, ground

Directions:

1. Grease a pan with the butter and spread cookie crumbs on the

bottom.

2. In a bowl, beat cream cheese with nutmeg, vanilla, rum and eggs,

whisk well and spread over the cookie crumbs.

3. Introduce in your air fryer and cook at 340 degrees F for 20

minutes.

4. Leave cheesecake to cool down and keep in the

fridge for 2 hours

before slicing and serving it.

Enjoy!

Nutrition: calories 412, fat 12, fiber 6, carbs 20,

protein 6

Strawberry Pie

Preparation time: 10 minutes Cooking time: 20

minutes **Servings**: 12

Ingredients:

For the crust:

1 cup coconut, shredded

1 cup sunflower seeds

¼ cup butter

For the filling:

1 teaspoon gelatin

8 ounces cream cheese

4 ounces strawberries

2 tablespoons water

½ tablespoon lemon juice

¼ teaspoon stevia

½ cup heavy cream

8 ounces strawberries, chopped for serving

Directions:

1. In your food processor, mix sunflower seeds with

coconut, a pinch

of salt and butter, pulse and press this on the bottom
of a cake pan

that fits your air fryer.

2. Heat up a pan with the water over medium heat,
add gelatin, stir

until it dissolves, leave aside to cool down, add this to
your food

processor, mix with 4 ounces strawberries, cream
cheese, lemon

juice and stevia and blend well.

3. Add heavy cream, stir well and spread this over
crust.

4. Top with 8 ounces strawberries, introduce in your
air fryer and

cook at 330 degrees F for 15 minutes.

5. Keep in the fridge until you serve it.

Enjoy!

Nutrition: calories 234, fat 23, fiber 2, carbs 6,
protein 7

Coffee Cheesecakes

Preparation time: 10 minutes Cooking time: 20 minutes **Servings**: 6

Ingredients:

For the cheesecakes:

2 tablespoons butter

8 ounces cream cheese

3 tablespoons coffee

3 eggs

1/3 cup sugar

1 tablespoon caramel syrup

For the frosting:

3 tablespoons caramel syrup

3 tablespoons butter

8 ounces mascarpone cheese, soft

2 tablespoons sugar

Directions:

1. In your blender, mix cream cheese with eggs, 2 tablespoons butter,

coffee, 1 tablespoon caramel syrup and 1/3 cup sugar and pulse

very well, spoon into a cupcakes pan that fits your air fryer,

introduce in the fryer and cook at 320 degrees F and bake for 20

minutes.

2. Leave aside to cool down and then keep in the freezer for 3 hours.

3. Meanwhile, in a bowl, mix 3 tablespoons butter with 3 tablespoons

caramel syrup, 2 tablespoons sugar and mascarpone, blend well,

spoon this over cheesecakes and serve them.

Enjoy!

Nutrition: calories 254, fat 23, fiber 0, carbs 21, protein 5

Cocoa Cookies

Preparation time: 10 minutes Cooking time: 14

minutes **Servings**: 12

Ingredients:

6 ounces coconut oil, melted

6 eggs

3 ounces cocoa powder

2 teaspoons vanilla

½ teaspoon baking powder

4 ounces cream cheese

5 tablespoons sugar

Directions:

1. In a blender, mix eggs with coconut oil, cocoa
powder, baking
powder, vanilla, cream cheese and swerve and stir
using a mixer.

2. Pour this into a lined baking dish that fits your air
fryer, introduce
in the fryer at 320 degrees F and bake for 14 minutes.

3. Slice cookie sheet into rectangles and serve.

Enjoy!

Nutrition: calories 178, fat 14, fiber 2, carbs 3, protein 5